Mythical Beasts

GIANTS AND TROLLS

Thanks to the creative team:
Senior Editor: Matthew Rake
Designer: Lauren Woods and collaborate agency

Hungry Tomato™
A division of Lerner Publishing Group, Inc.
241 First Avenue North
Minneapolis, MN 55401 USA

For reading levels and more information, look up this title at www.lernerbooks.com.

Main body text set in Galahad Std 12/1.5
Typeface provided by Adobe Systems.

Library of Congress Cataloging-in-Publication Data

Peebles, Alice.
    Giants and trolls / by Alice Peebles ; illustrated by Nigel Chilvers.
    pages cm. — (Mythical beasts)
      ISBN 978-1-4677-6340-0 (lb : alk. paper) —
    ISBN 978-1-4677-7653-0 (pb : alk. paper) —
    ISBN 978-1-4677-7217-4 (eb pdf)
      1. Giants—Juvenile literature. 2. Trolls—Juvenile literature.
    I. Chilvers, Nigel, illustrator. II. Title.
    BL820.G5P44 2016
    398'.45—dc23   2015001593

Manufactured in the United States of America
1 – VP – 7/15/15

ythical Beasts

GIANTS AND TROLLS

By Alice Peebles

Illustrated by Nigel Chilvers

HUNGRY
TOMATO™

Minneapolis

"His hair stood on end, and his mouth stretched wide open, showing sharp teeth flecked with fiery sparks."

Contents

Giants and Trolls

Meet the top ten biggest, meanest and most bloodthirsty creatures that stomped the world in ancient times . . .

Have you ever heard of Polyphemus, the fearsome Cyclops who had his one eye burned out by the Greek hero Odysseus? What about twelve-limbed Geryon, who fought to the death with Hercules? Or Cuchulain, a warrior of Irish folklore, who could actually grow in stature, spit out flecks of fire, and kill hundreds of men at a time?

Then there are the trolls, feared throughout Scandinavia for their massive size, ugly looks, and fondness for tasty humans. Up those bleak and windswept mountaintops of northern Europe, very near the realm of the Norse gods, you'll also find Hrungnir, the stone-headed giant who quarreled and fought with Thor himself. But who of these is the most ferocious of all? You're about to find out.

These ten beasts are shown
in vivid scenes that are based
on specific moments in their
stories . . . usually when they are
about to crush a much, much smaller
victim. The details about each monster
are inspired by mythology and folklore handed
down since ancient times. They appear in ranked
order of power from 1 to 10, with scores in that
range for each of five categories: Strength,
Repulsiveness, Special Powers, Ferocity, and
Invincibility. You'll also find a suggestion on
how to defeat or neutralize each mythical
foe. You, of course, are a lot more fortunate
than any victim and can take time to work
this out . . .

Are you ready to join Odysseus and his
crew as they face the fury of cannibal giants
or share the fate of a wretched captive at the
gloomy court of King Troll? Keep on reading to find
out more about just how nasty these giants can be . . .
and which of them would likely come out on top in a
ten-way fight to the death.

Wolf-Headed Humanoid
Cynocephalus

Teeth bared in a wolfish grin, Cynocephalus leaned over his catch as it roasted on the fire. He could not wait for the tasty pig to be cooked. He tore off a leg and was about to sink his long, pointed fangs into the pink meat when . . .

Suddenly, another of his kind bounded out of the trees and snatched the bone from his hand. The thief backed away, growling, slobbering, and chewing at the same time. Outraged, Cynocephalus leaped on his foe, howling and snapping at the flesh below the wolf's head. Soon they were writhing on the ground, fighting for supremacy . . . and meat.

How to defeat Cynocephalus

Cynocephalus's acute senses of sight and smell will alert him to any danger unless an opponent is very careful. The answer might be to prepare an animal trap, with a favorite prey as a lure, and make sure that he falls right in.

Where does this myth come from?

A race of fierce, dog-headed, human-like creatures was first recorded in 400 BCE by a Greek physician. The famous explorer Marco Polo also wrote about similar humanoids in the thirteenth century when he visited the island of Angamanain, now called the Andaman Islands, in the Bay of Bengal.

Beast
Power

Strength
5

Repulsiveness
1

Special Powers
2

Ferocity
6

Invincibility
6

Total
20/50

Three-In-One Warrior
Geryon

Stealthily, Hercules began driving the red cattle of Geryon down to the shore of their island home. He not only had to steal them but bring them back to his master, King Eurystheus. But a strange and mighty figure leaped in his path. It was the twelve-limbed, three-headed warrior, Geryon! Hercules could just see one of his three faces, twisted with fury.

His six arms flailing, Geryon rained down blows with sword and spear. Hercules leaped and dodged and parried with his shield. Slowly he maneuvered around so that the dazzling sun fell into Geryon's eyes, momentarily blinding the monster. In this brief moment, Hercules reached back and hurled his spear . . .

How to defeat Geryon

Like Hercules, an opponent would have to think of a clever trick to gain an advantage. An arrow dipped in the poisonous blood of a many-headed hydra would also do the job.

Where does this myth come from?

In Greek mythology, Geryon features in the 10th labor of Hercules, as recorded by Apollodorus of Athens and other writers. He was the son of Callirrhoe, a water nymph-goddess, and Chrysaor, who was himself the son of the monstrous Medusa. This perhaps explains Geryon's hideous looks and immense strength.

Beast
Power

Strength
6

Repulsiveness
2

Special Powers
1

Ferocity
7

Invincibility
6

Total
22/50

Fiend of the Forest
Forest Troll

One dark night a traveler plodded wearily through a forest far from home. Holding up his lantern, he saw a stone bridge ahead . . . and something else. A giant tree seemed to be moving toward him. Shocked, he saw it was a beast with branches growing from its head and shoulders. Its face grimaced, showing a single tooth. A forest troll! Its eyes glowed red in the lantern light and it lifted a stone mallet, ready to take aim. The traveler, too terrified to cry out, turned and fled, desperate to get away . . .

How to defeat a forest troll

Since trolls can't stand sunlight, they should be lured from their lairs in daytime, perhaps with the offer of money to cross their bridge or land. Then they will turn to stone.

Beast Power

Strength
7

Repulsiveness
6

Special Powers
1

Ferocity
7

Invincibility
5

Total
26/50

Where does this myth come from?

In the ancient language of Old Norse, the word troll *means "fiend" or "monster" and describes a kind of hostile, extremely ugly giant. Trolls occur in Icelandic legends and in western Scandinavian folklore. They were shape-shifters who often joined in human feasts and stole food. If you smelled cooking while out in the forest, you might be near a troll's dwelling.*

All-Seeing Herdsman
Argus

Many-eyed Argus burst into the satyr's hideout. "You'll steal no more cattle from us!" he roared.

Tossing aside a bone, the satyr fired off arrow after arrow at the giant's heart. But Argus, tall as a tree, batted them off like pine needles blowing in the wind. As he smashed his sword onto the satyr's skull, the creature reeled back.

Argus whirled him around and flung him against a column. The satyr was now a bloody blotch on the stone. With a grunt of satisfaction, Argus turned and strode back to his herds of plump, glossy cattle.

How to defeat Argus

Because Argus had so many eyes, some were always open and watchful. Only the god Hermes was able to lull Argus with music and storytelling until all of his one hundred eyes closed. Then Hermes struck the sleeping giant dead.

Where does this myth come from?

In Greek mythology, Argus was chosen by Hera, wife of the god Zeus, to guard a beautiful white heifer. This was really Io, a nymph Zeus loved. He had turned Io into a heifer to protect her from his jealous wife. After Argus was killed, Hera placed his eyes in the tail of her favorite bird, the peacock.

Beast Power

Strength
7

Repulsiveness
3

Special Powers
4

Ferocity
6

Invincibility
8

Total
28/50

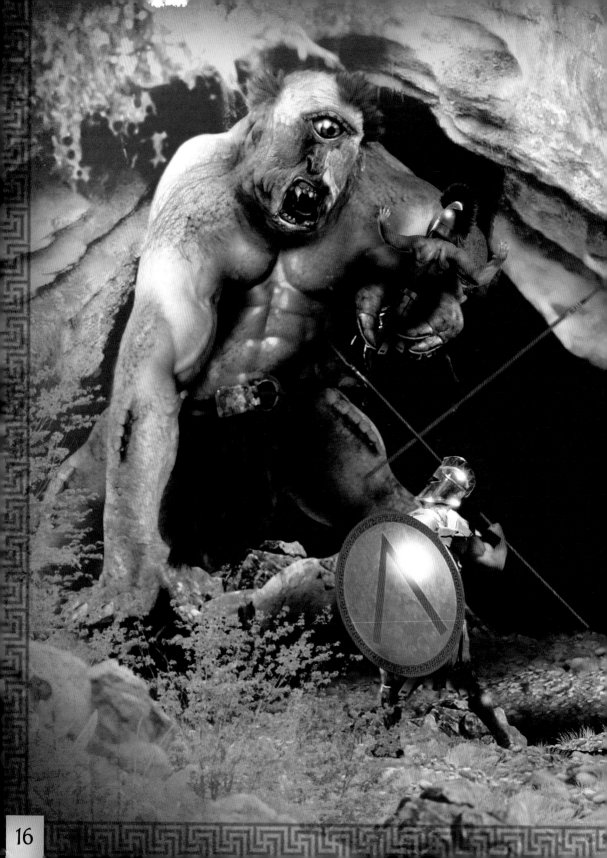

One-Eyed Colossus
Polyphemus

The Greek hero Odysseus and his warriors landed on the island of Sicily. Weary from their travels, they ventured into the hilltop cave of the one-eyed giant Polyphemus. All too soon, the giant came thundering up the hill. Spying the tiny strangers, he boomed, "Ha! Huuuumans!" Grabbing their weapons, the men scattered and tried to hide.

Two fled to the cave's entrance, but Polyphemus scooped one up, as if he were fishing a shrimp out of a pool. The giant clamped his crooked teeth around his victim, while the other warrior froze in horror. He knew his turn was next.

How to defeat Polyphemus

Odysseus defeated Polyphemus by blinding his one eye with a red-hot stake. Then Odysseus and his surviving men escaped. But to be completely safe, it might have been best to tie the giant up while he slumbered.

Where does this myth come from?

In Greek mythology, Polyphemus was the fiercest of the Cyclopes, a race of brutish, one-eyed giants. He was the son of the god Poseidon, ruler of the ocean, and has a cameo role in Homer's epic poem, the Odyssey. This story tells the adventures of Odysseus after the Trojan War. The blinding of Polyphemus enrages Poseidon, who makes Odysseus's journey long and hazardous.

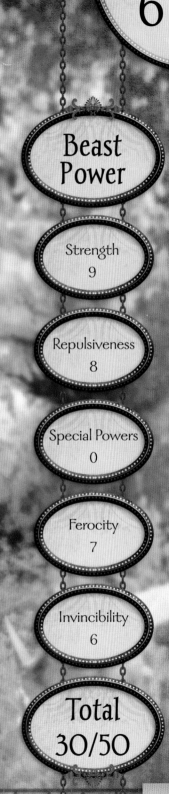

Beast Power

Strength
9

Repulsiveness
8

Special Powers
0

Ferocity
7

Invincibility
6

Total
30/50

Mountainous Savage
Mountain Troll

The mountaineer hauled himself up to a high ledge that seemed nearer to the sky than to the valley below. At once he was grabbed in a vice-like grip as an unearthly scream split his eardrums. "I shall eat your head before you have my treasure!"

A massive troll was lifting him in the air. Its tiny, bloodshot eyes rolled in fury and the troll was draped in chains of gold.

"No one climbs my mountain and lives!" roared the troll. Wriggling, the man peered down toward the troll's feet, where he could see human bones scattered about. Was this to be his fate?

―――――――❯•❮―――――――

How to defeat a mountain troll

A troll could not survive having his name shouted aloud, so he would be careful not to give it away. The trick would be to trick it out of him!

Where does this myth come from?

Troll tales abound in Norse mythology (the ancient tales of Scandinavia). In Norway especially, they are associated with the race of giants called Jötnar, who often warred with the gods. The word Trolleri means a kind of harmful magic, and trolls were thought to have the power to change themselves into storms, beasts, or even beautiful maidens.

5

Beast
Power

Strength
8

Repulsiveness
9

Special Powers
2

Ferocity
7

Invincibility
6

Total
32/50

Celtic Hero
Cuchulain

The battle fury was upon the mighty warrior Cuchulain. This fight with his opponent Ferdiad would decide an entire war. Cuchulain's magical strength took over. His muscles bulged, and his body seemed to grow to giant size. One eye swelled while the other shrank to a pinprick. His hair stood on end, and his mouth stretched wide open, showing sharp teeth flecked with fiery sparks.

Leaping in the air, he grasped his deadly spear, the *gae bolga*, and aimed. With a horrible crunch, the spear's barbed point hit Ferdiad's body just below his shield. Ferdiad fell lifeless to the ground as Cuchulain's men let out a deafening roar of triumph.

How to defeat Cuchulain

Dog meat can rob Cuchulain of his magical powers. He has to be tricked into eating it. This is exactly what happened when three witches disguised as old women invited him to share their stew. He then lost his great strength and was mortally wounded.

Where does this myth come from?

Cuchulain (pronounced KOO-kuhl-ihn) is a hero in many stories of Celtic folklore from Ireland. His father was a god or warrior and his mother an Ulster princess. His exploits bring him into contact with kings, queens, warriors, magicians, druids ,and sorceresses. Cuchulain's combat with Ferdiad decided the war between the armies of Ulster and Connaught.

Beast Power

Strength
8

Repulsiveness
7

Special Powers
4

Ferocity
8

Invincibility
8

Total
35/50

Cannibal Giants
Laestrygonians

Odysseus did not know that his ships had reached the island of a cannibal tribe called the Laestrygonians . . . until one of his scouts was grabbed and eaten by the king himself. The giants hurled boulders into the harbor, shattering Odysseus's ships like walnuts. Men dived overboard in terror.

But the Laestrygonians speared them like fish, carrying off the crews of eleven ships to make a tasty banquet. Odysseus and the crew of his own ship had no choice but to row away as quickly as possible . . .

How to defeat Laestrygonians

Avoid them! These cannibals won't last long without a food source. A captive of a single giant could also try a sleeping potion.

Where does this myth come from?

These pitiless monsters of Greek mythology occur in Homer's Odyssey and cause the most disastrous episode of Odysseus's wanderings. The harbor where his ships are anchored is very narrow and sheltered, making them easy targets for the bloodthirsty giants. Only Odysseus and the crew of his own ship escape with their lives.

Beast Power

Strength
9

Repulsiveness
6

Special Powers
2

Ferocity
10

Invincibility
9

Total
36/50

Giant of Ice and Stone
Hrungnir

As Hrungnir and Thor faced each other, lightning split the sky and thunder boomed over the mountaintops. The god stood waist-high to the stone-headed, stone-hearted giant. But Thor's courage was legendary.

"Your puny sound effects don't frighten ME!" yelled Hrungnir. Thor laughed. He whirled his magic hammer, Mjollnir, around his head, then let it fly at the very moment the giant hurled his whetstone.

The hammer crashed into the whetstone in midair, shattering it into razor-sharp pieces of flint. And Mjollnir whirred onward, toward the huge stone head of Hrungnir . . .

How to defeat Hrungnir

Without a magic hammer, only a clever trick could vanquish Hrungnir. He could be lured to a cliff overlooking a lake to admire his stone face in the water. Then, if he leaned over far enough, it might be possible to push him right in.

Where does this myth come from?

Hrungnir's story is part of the legends of Norse mythology. This episode was recounted in the thirteenth century in a famous work called the Prose Edda *by an Icelandic poet and chieftain, Snorri Sturluson. The mightiest giant of the icy Northern realms, Hrungnir once declared he could kill all the gods of Asgard. So Thor challenged him to a single combat . . .*

Beast Power

Strength
10

Repulsiveness
4

Special Powers
6

Ferocity
8

Invincibility
9

Total
37/50

Ruler of all Trolls
King Troll

To the trolls, it sounded like squeaking, but the man was really shrieking at the top of his voice as they dragged him before their king. He stopped yelling as his eyes took in the looming shape of King Troll. The legs were as thick as tree trunks, the hands ended in yellow claws, and below a mane of matted hair was an ancient face seamed with furrows and a snarling mouth.

Licking his lips with a black tongue, King Troll grabbed the man and prepared to roast him on the fire. The other trolls squealed and capered about. How long before one more skull hung from the king's belt of trophies?

How to defeat King Troll

Salt is one way to get rid of trolls. It was thought to have magical powers that were stronger than those of the trolls. But King Troll would probably need a barrelful rather than a pinch!

Where does this myth come from?

A troll king, or "old man of the mountains," appears in a play called Peer Gynt *by the Norwegian dramatist Henrik Ibsen. The play was inspired by a Norwegian fairy tale featuring trolls, brownies, gnomes, and witches. The troll king is called Dovregubben. He lives inside the Dovre Mountains with his court.*

Beast Power

Strength
9

Repulsiveness
9

Special Powers
3

Ferocity
8

Invincibility
9

Total
38/50

Rogues' Gallery

10 Cynocephalus

20

This dog-headed species was thought to live in India and North Africa. Some people think they were related to werewolves.

9 Geryon

22

The three-headed monster had a monster-hound called Orthrus. It had two heads and was the brother of Cerberus, guard dog of the Underworld.

6 Polyphemus

30

The Cyclops devoured four more of Odysseus's men before the others escaped. Then he flung huge rocks at their boat as they rowed away.

5 Mountain Troll

32

Rich mountain trolls who hoarded treasure might take it out to air and, just to be doubly safe, have a bull or snake guard it.

2 Hrungnir

37

The shattering of Hrungnir's whetstone was followed by the smashing of his head by Thor's hammer Mjollnir. The giant crashed down on top of Thor, pinning the god to the ground. Thor was unable to move, even with the help of two other gods. Only his young son Magni was strong enough to lift up the dead giant and free Thor.

8

Forest Troll

Besides having twigs and branches instead of hair, this troll could morph into a log or a tree stump. It could also make itself invisible.

7

Argus

The giant used his superhuman strength to kill a rampaging bull and an even more destructive foe: the half-nymph, half-serpent Echidna.

4

Cuchulain

The king gave Cuchulain his own special weapons, since the warrior was so strong that all other swords and spears broke in his huge hands.

3

Laestrygonians

Odysseus's scouts first met the hideous queen of the Laestrygonians. She called for her husband, who tore one of the men in two and drank his blood.

1

King Troll

Once, Thor himself was lured to the huge mountain castle of the troll king Geirrodur. Here in the great hall, the troll snatched a piece of white-hot metal from the fire and flung it at Thor. The god caught it in his iron gloves and hurled it straight back. It burned right through an iron pillar, the troll king himself, and the castle wall behind him.

Want to Know More?

Trollery, Drollery

In Scandinavian folklore, the phrase "being taken to the mountain" was code for being snatched by trolls. A spiteful troll might tell a captive, "Get out!" and allow the person to try to escape . . . before trying finally to skewer the fleeing captive. People who did get away and managed to return home might have lost their memory or their sanity.

Church bells rung long and loud could make a troll fall gravely ill, giving a captive a chance to get away. The the death-by-naming technique was another popular way to vanquish trolls. A maiden captured by a troll called Dunker managed to do this. When she named him, he exploded and the mountain around him collapsed, leaving her free to go home.

Norwegian trolls were the biggest of all and had a variety of ugly features, such as a big, flat nose (or a long, thin one), a crooked back, huge feet, over-long teeth, and leathery, scaly, or hairy skin. Sometimes a troll had more than one head, or an extra eye in the middle of the forehead.

Many Scandinavian landmarks have the word *troll* in them. For example, the *troldeskoven* or troll forests in Denmark are known for their ancient bent and twisted trees. Their strange shapes were caused by wind and frost. Wander there at sunset and maybe you'll see a troll!

Boomerang Hammer

Thor and the other Norse gods possessed many magical weapons and equipment. Thor's hammer, Mjollnir, was forged by two dwarf brothers. The trickster god Loki bet them his head that they could not make a hammer to outclass Odin's marvelous spear Gungnir.

They accepted the bet, but as they worked, Loki turned himself into a fly and stung one of the dwarfs to distract him. The hammer's handle ended up shorter than it should have been, so the hammer could only be wielded with one hand. But the gods voted it the most wonderful weapon of all. Not only could it smash through mountains, but it always hit its target and returned to the hand of Thor.

And Loki? He wriggled out of losing his head by saying his neck was not part of the deal and the dwarfs could not possibly avoid cutting off the tiniest part of his neck. Instead one of the dwarfs sewed his lips together to keep him quiet . . . for a change.

Labors of Hercules

Strong heroes often get tangled up with monsters that no one else can defeat. One of the most famous monster-slayers of myth is the Greek hero Hercules, who was given twelve almost-impossible tasks to perform by his master, King Eurystheus. Hercules was actually the son of Zeus, so no wonder he had special powers.

Many of his labors involved killing or capturing animals, as with the cattle of Geryon. Probably the stinkiest task was cleaning out the stables used by thousands of cattle belonging to King Augeas. They were piled high with dung which had not been cleared away for decades. The challenge was to clean up all this mess in a day. Hercules did so by diverting two nearby rivers to run through the stables and carry off the filth in one mighty, fast-running torrent. Since then the phrase "cleaning out the Augean stables" has often been used to describe a horrible, grubby job of giant proportions.

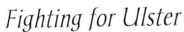

Fighting for Ulster

Cuchulain had his very first adventure as a seven-year-old boy. King Conchobar of Ulster had a band of boy warriors and Cuchulain wanted to join them. To prove himself, he knocked them down one by one in single combat until they submitted to his leadership.

One day, he came racing home from battle in his chariot, drawn by the twin horses that had been born on the day of his own birth.

He had hung the heads of three foes from the chariot and was still frenzied with battle fury. To calm his rage, the king's warriors dipped him in three tubs of ice-cold water. The first one burst, the second boiled, but the third just got warm. So Cuchulain was perfectly cool again!

Index

)●●(

The Author

Alice Peebles is an editor and writer specializing in the arts and humanities for children. She is a coauthor of *Encyclopedia of Art for Young People* and one of the creators of *The Guzunder Gang* audiobook series. She has also edited and written for several children's magazines focused on history, art, and geography. She lives in London, England.

The Artist

Nigel Chilvers is a digital illustrator based in the United Kingdom. He has illustrated numerous children's books.